Bridges into lea
for adults who find
provision hard to reach

DEVELOPING ADULT TEACHING AND LEARNING: PRACTITIONER GUIDES

Yvon Appleby

niace
promoting adult learning

National Institute of Adult Continuing Education
(England and Wales)

21 De Montfort Street
Leicester LE1 7GE

Company registration no. 2603322
Charity registration no. 1002775
Published by NIACE in association with NRDC

NIACE has a broad remit to promote lifelong learning opportunities for adults.
NIACE works to develop increased participation in education and training,
particularly for those who do not have easy access because of class, gender, age,
race, language and culture, learning difficulties or disabilities, or insufficient
financial resources.

For a full catalogue of all NIACE's publications visit
www.niace.org.uk/publications

Cataloguing in Publication Data
A CIP record for this title is available from the British Library
ISBN 978-1-86201-340-7

Cover design by Creative by Design Limited, Paisley
Designed and typeset by Creative by Design Limited, Paisley
Printed and bound by Latimer Trend

Developing adult teaching and learning: Practitioner guides

This is one of two practitioner guides arising from the longitudinal study of Adult Learners' Lives, carried out at Lancaster University from 2002 to 2005. This study was part of the National Research and Development Centre for Adult Literacy and Numeracy (NRDC)'s programme of research into economic development and social inclusion. The other practitioner guide arising from this study is entitled *Responding to people's lives*, by Yvon Appleby and David Barton.

These guides illuminate the value of a 'social practices' approach to adult teaching and learning, whereby developing skills is part of a wider, holistic way for teachers and other professionals to make learning and achievement relevant and meaningful to learners' everyday lives. They offer practical ideas about how to work with adults in a variety of settings, taking into account their life patterns, circumstances, future plans and hopes.

For more information on the Adult Learners' Lives project, please see
http://www.nrdc.org.uk

Contents

Acknowledgements

Many people have contributed to the fieldwork, research collaborations and ideas represented here. I would like to thank colleagues on the NRDC Adult Learners' Lives (ALL) project, Roz Ivanič, Rachel Hodge, Karin Tusting and particularly David Barton for his support in writing this guide. We are indebted to all those in the community organisations whom we worked with, particularly the learners who shared their individual lives and stories with us.

The book has benefited from collaborations in the field and in later discussion with managers, trainers and practitioners from across the North West of England. Thanks to them for their insightful contributions, generous commitment and critical reading. In particular thanks to Linda Foster, Steve Thompson, Kath Moffatt, Shahla Holgeth, Jeannette Fowler, Julie Collins, Catherine Peel and Meriel Lobley.

Thanks also to the NRDC critical readers for their helpful comments: Nuala Broderick, Cathie Clarke, Tim Deignan, Sue McCulloch, Carole Smith and Jo Wellings.

Thanks also for additional comment, advice and editorial work from Alison Wedgbury, Ursula Howard and Paula Teo.

Summary of conclusions

These are the key messages for practice arising from NRDC's Adult Learners' Lives (ALL) research project for those teaching and supporting excluded groups of literacy, language and numeracy (LLN) learners in community settings.

For providers

- Formal learning may often be out of the reach of some people: it is not the potential learners who are 'hard to reach', but providers who are hard to reach by potential learners.
- Adult LLN needs to be structured to work well within specific, and varied community settings, supporting people dealing with complex factors in their lives.
- Flexible, achievable timescales and progression routes need to reflect learners' challenging circumstances, needs and aspirations.
- Providers and teachers should be aware of and respond flexibly to learners' changing patterns of life and their readiness or not to attend and persist in learning. This is defined by learners as 'the right time' to learn.

For teachers

- LLN teaching needs to take advantage of people's existing skills, competencies, passions and talents and link those with wider curriculum opportunities.
- LLN teaching in the community can complement the new networks of support that vulnerable people have started to access.
- Teachers can help tie a sense of future into learning to enable people to hold on to a longer-term purpose, and sustain a feeling that they have something worth aiming for.
- LLN teachers can be the bridge that helps learners to move between different types of provision at appropriate stages.

For teacher-educators and staff development managers

- When planning the content of LLN initial teacher training and continuing professional development (CPD), teacher-educators should work with specialists in different types of community support, to include a focus on community learning.

- LLN teachers working in community settings should have opportunities for networking and access to mentors who have expertise in community learning.

For funders

- Funding should prioritise outreach work by 'joined up' services and multi-agency working to engage vulnerable people who experience turbulence, hardship and complex circumstances in their lives.

- Sufficient resources should be available to maintain the flexibility, security and quality of community LLN provision.

- People with the least material resources need support in meeting specific costs, such as travel and childcare, that enable them to progress in learning.

How the guide is organised

The guide is organised in three sections:

- Introduction
- Guidelines for working in community settings (with case studies of four learners)
- Supporting adult literacy, numeracy and ESOL teaching in community settings.

Each section contributes to the overall focus: understanding the critical issues involved in working with learners in community settings in adult LLN provision. All sections look at how such provision can differ from other types in different settings, and discuss the things that need to be taken into account in working with people described as 'hard to reach' or as 'vulnerable' learners. Each section questions what these terms mean and explores the challenges and implications of working in this way.

Finally, there is a list of suggested further reading and web-based resources.

1 Introduction: Being able to participate in a communication-rich society

Having the resources to function in a society that uses a range of methods and media of communication (including reading, writing and speaking) provides the possibility of being included. Not having them makes participation more difficult and may result in, or add to, social exclusion.

Providing learning opportunities for people within the government priority groups,[1] outlined in the UK Skills for Life strategy (DfEE, 2001), requires an approach that is based upon reaching out to support learning in community settings, supporting people wherever they live. This approach builds upon understanding and good practice developed from joining up community education, community development, the voluntary sector, organisations dealing with social and health issues, and lifelong learning.

This guide is about adult LLN provision which is offered in a range of community settings outside of the further education (FE) sector and workplace learning, or even more mainstream adult community learning. Provision in these settings is sometimes described as working with people who are 'hard to reach' or 'vulnerable' and least likely to attend formal provision.

This guide identifies practical steps for practitioners, managers, funders and those supporting initial training and professional development. It draws on recent research and on collaborations with many practitioners working in community settings who have contributed their ideas and experience.

We use the generic term 'teacher' throughout the guide, although we recognise that different terms may be used in different settings to describe this role, including 'tutor' and 'trainer'.

In this guide we use a social practice approach that sees literacy, numeracy and ESOL skills as always connected to learners' purposes and daily lives (for further discussion see Barton and Hamilton, 2000 and Papen, 2005).

---

[1]The priority groups include unemployed people and benefit claimants, prisoners, public sector employees, people in low-skilled employment and other groups at risk of social exclusion including people who live in disadvantaged communities.

Adult LLN in different settings with different learners

Learning can fit into daily life
Library photo, posed by models ©*www.JohnBirdsall.co.uk*

What counts as language, literacy and numeracy, and the significance attributed to them, may change, both in individual lives and in policy (see Hamilton and Hillier, 2006). In individual lives, this may mean becoming computer literate for work, recreation and pleasure. In policy, LLN skills have become a significant part of the national agenda in the UK as part of the Skills for Life strategy designed to support employability and social cohesion. This has changed the landscape of provision and has created new patterns of delivery for adult LLN. As a result of these changes, affected by and responding to changes in funding, there are both 'gaps and overlaps' in provision and providers. Some new providers, such as the probation service and regeneration agencies, are offering literacy, numeracy and ESOL learning in community settings embedded within their wider service provision. This has been made possible by funding for Skills for Life delivery. At the same time, other providers working in community settings with 'hard to reach' groups have sought alternatives to adult LLN funding, finding constraints to the flexibility of learning opportunities they are able to offer to particular clients or service users. They have 'opted out' of Skills for Life, seeking money from sources such as The Big Lottery Fund in order to offer a wider range of flexible learning.

A significant change created by the national strategy is that organisations providing support services for adults in community settings are now involved in the delivery of Skills for Life where previously they may have offered a range of community education in which LLN were embedded programmes. Additionally, many of those who have delivered adult LLN in the college sector are increasingly involved in the delivery of Skills for Life in community settings. As the range of learning environments has increased, teaching has built upon the tacit knowledge of other professionals such as community development workers and advice workers, as well as those from the voluntary and community sector. It builds upon existing models of working with individuals as whole people and often within the context of their everyday lives in networks, families and communities. The approach is therefore not new although the specific focus on LLN may be.

The research: looking at literacy and learning in people's lives

The material for this guide comes from the NRDC Adult Learners' Lives (ALL) project, carried out at Lancaster University between 2002 and 2005. In the first phase we looked at literacy, numeracy and ESOL learning in college classes, to understand connections between what people gained from these learning contexts and how it related to their everyday lives (see Ivanič, Appleby, Hodge, Tusting and Barton, 2006). This work is developed in *Responding to people's lives*, another title in this series of practitioner guides.

In the second phase, the focus of this guide, we worked in community settings in Blackburn, Liverpool and Lancaster to understand the experiences of people attending a wide range of adult LLN learning in community settings (Barton, Appleby, Hodge, Tusting and Ivanič, 2006). We wanted to know if and how this type of provision differed from college-based provision because of the context of delivery. In each place we worked in a number of settings where adult literacy and numeracy was being provided in a range of different ways. These included educational programmes provided by college-based specialists, through to informal learning by means of participation in activities within organisations. From the most to the least formal, these were:

Pandion Hall: a drug and alcohol support centre that offered one-to-one support and group-based structured day programmes. The educational activities included literacy, communications and IT and distance literacy and numeracy courses delivered in partnership with the local learndirect centre.

The Big Issue: a national organisation for homeless people offering a range of support services. The site we worked in offered support for health, housing and income generation by selling *The Big Issue* magazine. The learning centre offered a range of educational provision including music, gardening, cooking, literacy, numeracy and IT.

Safespace: a shelter for homeless young people in a town in the North West of England catering for those in need of accommodation and support. The shelter worked with an associated day centre that offered informal education on a needs basis. The young people were offered a selection of learning and guidance opportunities in an informal environment that related to both their immediate circumstances as well as their future plans.

Midway Tenants' Association: run by volunteers on a previously owned council estate in a large city. The association provided a community-based resource for advice, support and activities for a range of ages. The 'office' provided informal IT learning, Internet access and information and support to attend formal college programmes.

Emerge: a local domestic violence support group working on the outskirts of a large city. The organisation provided support and advice for those with experience of domestic violence, helping women to navigate complex legal and bureaucratic systems whilst maintaining a safe environment. It offered a range of learning activities and supported some women to attend college programmes.

Researching in community settings

First, each of these organisations offered a range of support relating to its core service provision, from drug and alcohol support to individual and community safety. Each also provided some form of learning, whether informal or formal, as part of this work. Providing adult LLN learning opportunities, within the work of these organisations, responded to two factors relating to national changes created by the Skills for Life strategy. Firstly, organisations offering formal learning opportunities, such as Pandion Hall and the Big Issue, used new funding to deliver what may previously have been termed adult basic education. As funding has been channelled into discrete LLN targets and qualifications, community organisations have responded by adapting what they offer to contain more recognisable Skills for Life content.

Second, all the organisations, including those offering the most informal learning, have become more aware of the need for LLN skills through government media campaigns that stress the link between such skills and employability. Organisations that want to support social inclusion and financial independence increasingly see the need to provide learning opportunities – LLN – as part of this work. In the case of Emerge and Safespace this included supporting people to become financially independent and to be able to take control of their lives. All of the organisations also recognised that the people they worked with had overwhelmingly negative experiences of school and authority, which often affected their educational and social confidence. Supporting these people to become confident across a range of adult learning programmes was therefore an important aspect of their work.

These two factors have created a change in the type and range of LLN provision in many organisations that work with people in community settings. The way that this has been integrated, adapted and delivered in each organisation depends on several factors, including the main focus of service provision and support offered, the reasons people have for attending (voluntarily or in compliance with an order) and the existing types of provision offered. In each research site we spent a great deal of time talking to people and getting to understand the organisation, what their main focus of support they offered was and the various people associated with it. Many organisations were themselves part of wider networks of support and systems of inter-agency delivery.

A social perspective that recognises people and their lives

A social practice approach recognises that some people lead settled lives, with varying degrees of control over their actions, whilst others experience turbulence[2] with little control at all. This approach starts with the everyday meanings, and the practical and social applications of LLN, recognising that people, whatever their circumstances, learn and develop necessary skills and desired strategies for themselves. A social practice approach supports collaborative learning that takes account of people's lives both inside and outside the classroom. It provides the possibility for a democratic model of adult LLN learning that promotes 'really useful' knowledge. It also supports social participation by recognising and developing knowledge and skills to support what people are dealing with in their lives and the strategies they require to manage these.

---

[2] Reder (2004) uses the term turbulence to describe the lack of control and unpredictability in some people's lives.

Learners' life issues may include:

- being homeless
- being part of a moving population (e.g. refugees, asylum seekers and homeless people)
- experiencing violence, racism or homophobia
- experiencing physical and mental health issues
- dealing with drug or alcohol addiction or misuse
- dealing with legal or care orders
- dealing with poverty.

People who are dealing with some, or a combination, of the factors above are frequently identified as 'at risk' learners. This term is used to describe people who are 'at risk' of social exclusion through non-participation in education. A social practice approach recognises the links between people's lives and learning, especially the successful learning that often occurs outside the classroom. It explains the difficulty that some people have fitting in with what they may see as inflexible mainstream adult learning.

Five principles of social practice teaching

In *Responding to people's lives* (Appleby and Barton, 2008), another title in this practitioner guide series, we outline five principles of a social practice approach to teaching:

- **Research everyday practices:** Teachers and learners can investigate their changing literacy practices and the learning practices which support them.
- **Take account of learners' lives:** People are complex; they have their own histories, identities, current circumstances and imagined futures. We need to engage with different aspects of people's lives in a teaching and learning relationship.
- **Learning by participation:** Using authentic materials, in tasks for real purposes, helps to make helpful links between learning and literacy, numeracy and language in people's everyday lives and support learning progress.
- **Learning in safe, supported contexts:** Recognising and valuing the social aspects of learning, including physical and emotional safety and respect.
- **Locate literacy learning in other forms of meaning-making:** Recognising and working with different literacies that include oral, visual, individual and group ways of communicating.

These principles are designed to support reflection on the complexities of adult LLN teaching and learning. They are based upon a view that teaching and learning are more than 'broadcasting' and 'transmitting' information or knowledge. They are also based upon what people think, feel and bring to learning, and thus nearly always have a social dimension. These are general principles that can be applied to most teaching and learning contexts, including those which take place in community settings.

Whilst there are areas of overlap, there are significant differences in LLN programmes offered in community settings. This guide describes some of the key issues that need to be addressed in each of these learning environments and shows some of the differences which teachers need to take into account. It builds upon what we outline as general 'guidelines for a social practice approach' and demonstrates ways of using and developing these within teaching adult LLN in community settings.

2 Guidelines for working in community settings: Four learners, four lives

Lives and learning in community settings

People who come to classes are more than just learners. We do not immediately know fully why they have chosen to attend, what their previous experiences have been and what they really want from participating. Not many people wish to repeat situations in which they feel inadequate or which create anxiety. Where there is an overriding positive outcome as a result of learning, such as achieving promotion at work, it is a risk worth taking. Where the risk attached to learning outweighs the possibility of any visible positive outcome, or change in circumstances, it is understandable that people may be less willing to engage in formal learning. Community educators and community workers have used informal learning as a way of engaging people in learning within the contexts of their lives, and sometimes also to provide a link to more formal learning (McNeil and Dixon, 2005).

As many community workers and community educators understand, where people are managing difficult or complex situations in turbulent lives, the type of learning and methods of teaching offered must be made relevant and sustainable for them. This may involve exploring the tensions and possibilities of working in the community to provide a range of learning opportunities that support social inclusion (Deer Richardson and Wolfe, 2004; see also Tett, 2006). Outreach work may also be needed: as adult LLN provision has become formalised in England, it is important to recognise where this still excludes some people.

From our research in community settings (Barton, Appleby, Hodge, Tusting and Ivanič, 2006; McNeil and Dixon, 2005) we found that some adults find some provision 'out of their reach' because:

- it does not take account of their immediate need for survival and safety
- it is offered at the wrong time or in the wrong place for them
- it too closely resembles previous negative experiences of learning and authority

- the pace of learning is too fast or does not allow for breaks in learning resulting from health issues or changes in life circumstances
- there is inadequate practical or emotional support to attend consistently
- it is difficult to see the relevance and end result of learning in relation to current circumstances.

Whilst these factors need to be recognised in any adult learning environment, they are essential in community settings. From these insights, our overall findings and ongoing work with practitioners, we have developed four principles to support working in community settings.

Four guidelines to support working in community settings

- **Take account of people's current circumstances and responsibilities:** Often, immediate concerns for safety or survival have to take precedence over learning. It has to be the 'right time' to participate in learning that is meaningful and relevant to changing life circumstances. For some people, attending provision is about safety and daily structure, and for others, it is about achieving goals and moving on in their life.

- **Take account of people's barriers to learning:** These can include physical, mental, social and emotional issues in life circumstances where people experience turbulence. Some people have past or current experiences of violence and trauma which are not always visible or expressed. These are both a part of their history and affect their current circumstances as well as their future.

- **Take account of people's feelings of social exclusion:** Whilst people may feel excluded, and have negative experiences of authority and of learning, they may also have similar purposes and aspirations as most people with regards to health, jobs, family and becoming settled.

- **Recognise and build on people's existing skills, competencies and interests:** These may be unrelated to formal learning and can include activities such as songwriting, poetry, using the internet, friendships, supporting others or finding out information on health, children's education, legal matters or benefits.

Working with the guidelines to support learning in community settings

The starting point of these four guidelines is that people who fit the Skills for Life priority groups are often far from being reluctant learners. They can make enormous efforts to mediate between their challenging life circumstances and engagement in learning. We can see this clearly in the four lives in this section. If we measured success in learning solely in terms of a qualification achieved, regular attendance and progression, each one's achievement might be considered small. However, if we take a broader and longer-term view and include the challenges each person is dealing with, then the progress and achievements that are made over time and in many aspects of their lives become more striking.

We therefore need to link people's lives with their learning, and include their life histories, multiple identities, current life circumstances and possible futures. For both teachers and learners, these factors affect how we are seen, see ourselves and shape the day-to-day fabric of life. This is what people bring to any learning context. Even where they are not consciously recognised or acknowledged, they are part of their relationship to learning. The four guidelines provide ways of seeing people beyond the parameters of formal education and qualification targets. Instead, they locate people's achievements in the context of their particular lives. This is particularly important when working with people who may be dealing with difficult and complex issues, feel different from their peers or feel socially excluded. By looking at people through the guidelines we offer, we recognise that each learner has:

- a particular life history
- a current way of life and identities
- life circumstances and significant events
- hopes and aspirations for the future.

To show how this approach supports our guidelines, we now discuss four examples of people we have worked with.

Example of Guideline 1: Take account of people's current circumstances and responsibilities

The example of Caroline, who attended Pandion Hall, shows how the issues that she was dealing with shaped her current circumstances and responsibilities.

Library photo, posed by models ©Dragan Trifunovic/Shutterstock

Caroline was in her late 40s when we met her, at a time when she regularly attended the Structured Day Programme at Pandion Hall. She had been good at school, coming top of the class with good reports, but became fed up in her last year, and wanted to leave. By this time she had started going out and drinking, and got married at 20 and had two children. Although she trained and got a good secretarial job, she had to leave because of childcare difficulties. After this she ended up with unskilled work and what she called 'daft jobs' like factory work.

After moving to a new area and going through marriage difficulties and a divorce, Caroline married again. After three children from her new marriage, she divorced her second husband: she drank continually and was violent. She described this time as the worst in her life, when she would drop the kids off at school and then drink in public areas all day. As her health deteriorated she was referred to a local detox unit – which she has now attended over 20 times. She has also been in unsuccessful short-term residential as well as more successful longer-term structured rehabilitation programmes. When she returns home she faces the same issues. The structure and activities provided at Pandion Hall enable Caroline to have something to think about other than drinking. This, she said, has saved her life.

Caroline had always wanted to learn, but when she attended college she felt different to people who talked about their families, hobbies and recent consumer purchases. She was unable to tell anyone about her alcohol dependency and the pressure meant that she drank to be able to manage her anxiety this caused. She found learning with 'normal' people difficult. By contrast, Pandion Hall provided a secure and non-pressurised environment where she was more able to succeed at her own pace whilst managing lapses of drinking. She managed to do courses in IT, art, creative writing and music technology. With her growing confidence, she decided to try college again, especially as the tutor on the structured programme, whom she liked and trusted, also taught in her local college.

Caroline's everyday literacy and numeracy practices

Although Caroline's current circumstances and responsibilities made accessing learning difficult whilst she managed her alcohol dependency, she regularly used literacy and numeracy skills in her everyday life. She had a good grasp of writing from her secretarial work which meant that she was able to express herself creatively as well as help her children with their schoolwork. These skills also meant that she was able to tackle IT courses offered, adding to her existing knowledge and confidence.

As a single parent, she used numeracy skills to manage the family budget, making decisions about long- and short-term strategies for survival. These skills were also important in managing her rehabilitation programmes. Caroline saw herself as someone who could read, write and manage everyday literacy and numeracy. The skills that she particularly wanted to improve were personal and social confidence, so that she could manage to hold her life together enough to attend college and continue with her learning.

Current ways of life and identities clearly influence the type, place and pace of learning that it is possible to participate in. Programmes which learners are currently engaged in create possibilities and constraints and affect identities: who we think we are and how other people see us. Caroline's life shows how an early life history does not result in current practices and identities in a casual way: whilst often related, the relationship between past and present is not simple. Caroline had a positive early school career. It was only as an adult facing relationship breakdown and marital domestic violence that she experienced overwhelming difficulties in her life.

People may not able to participate or concentrate on learning when they feel unsafe, are concerned with finding a bed for the night, have difficulty managing their medication or authorised drug regime or are worried about going to court. There is often a time that is 'right' for learning, when people are able to manage some of the difficult factors in their life enough to participate, engage and succeed. This could be associated with a new relationship, responding to a new key worker, moving to a new area or gaining control over a 'habit'.

People who are managing difficult factors in their lives told us that having a place to go that provided structure and safety was an important part of being able to learn. This is not easily provided in formal education. Safety meant not facing negativity or abuse – whether verbal or physical – from either teachers or other learners. It also meant being safe from harassment on the streets, in violent relationships and within some 'user communities'.

Implications for teaching and learning

The experiences of Caroline and many of the other people attending Pandion Hall suggest that providers of formal learning opportunities should review how well they respond to and accommodate learners' needs and circumstances, beyond a focus on specific skills and qualifications in recommended timescales.

We see that, in community settings:

- **Learning can provide a safe and structured space.** For some, their main motivation and the benefits of Pandion Hall were the structure and routine it offered as they tried to restructure their lives and deal with alcohol or drug dependency.

- **Learning has to be at the 'right time'.** The 'right time' indicates having achieved some control over one's life circumstances, and that what is being learned is relevant and useful. People's needs have to take precedence over pressures to achieve specific learning outcomes. Provision should also allow that several attempts may need to be made.

- **Immediate concerns with safety and survival must be recognised:** people have to focus on these above all else. For learners such as those at Pandion Hall, finding a place to sleep, food, clean needles or a safe house away from violence take precedence.

All of the service providers we worked with focused on people's futures as well as dealing with the immediate issues. Where this sense of future was tied into learning, it enabled learners to grasp a longer-term purpose more firmly, so that in spite of difficulties there was a feeling of something worth aiming for. For Caroline, this enabled her to move from saying she didn't ever want to go to college to attending a mainstream college course within a matter of months.

Example of Guideline 2: Take account of individual barriers to learning

Individual barriers to learning can be changeable, interrelated and complex, as Sophie's experiences show.

Library photo, posed by model
©coka/Shutterstock

Sophie was 18 years old and regularly attended Safespace, a shelter for homeless people. Her early life had been unsettled as her mother, a teacher, was alcohol- and drug-dependent. She hated school, although she was very bright, and ended up being expelled because of violent behaviour and arson. She became homeless at 15 years old, failing her GCSEs. She had attended college but because of the pressure of being homeless and coping with substance misuse she only managed to 'dip in and out' rather than attend regularly.

Whilst living at Safespace Sophie attended the associated day centre as somewhere to go, to meet people and to get food. She did not like attending the drug and alcohol advice session and found the basic skills session boring and unrewarding. Instead, she enjoyed reading, particularly her favourite author Virginia Andrews, as she felt her books were about real life. She also liked creative writing and wrote *haiku* poetry in both French and English to give her something to focus on. Sophie's pregnancy added to some of the immediate housing and substance-related difficulties that she was dealing with.

Towards the end of the our research, Sophie gave birth to a baby girl and was in better health. She was able to move out of the mother and baby unit. She moved into her sister's flat as a temporary measure whilst trying to find an independent space for herself and the baby. She was determined to continue with her studies and had hoped to eventually study veterinary medicine or psychology.

Sophie's everyday literacy and numeracy practices

Sophie used writing as a form of self-expression and enjoyed the challenge of writing *haiku* poetry. She also participated in many of the arts activities offered at Safespace, including those using computer graphics and IT. She used numeracy in managing her money and searching for accommodation. She used both literacy and numeracy in a range of ways, from managing her drug dependency to keeping in regular contact with friends by texting.

Not all adults with a negative experience of school see themselves as an 'educational failure', as Caroline and Sophie illustrate. Sophie knew, and clearly articulated, what she wanted to learn, as well as what she did not.

The barriers to learning in Sophie's life were physical, emotional and social. She was homeless, dealing with substance misuse, pregnant and facing the future as a young single mother. Some of these barriers were compounded by having insufficient practical resources; others, by the continuing turbulence in her life.

Implications for teaching and learning

Like Sophie, many of the people we worked with had histories of pain, trauma, violence and ill health. Their early family lives often contained experiences of being unsettled, shifting and not belonging. Violence, bullying and intimidation from both within families and outside – in school, neighbourhoods and local communities – were common experiences. There were also many examples of being physically and mentally abused by those with caring responsibilities. Jenny

Horsman (2000) has discussed the impact of trauma and violence on individuals, showing the need for teachers to recognise this sometimes hidden aspect of adult learners' lives.

Difficulties at school, illustrated by Sophie, frequently leads to difficulties with authority in other areas of life. Authority at home, at school, through social services and the criminal justice system is often felt to be unfair, punitive and against an individual's sense of justice. People often feel categorised, stigmatised and made invisible by systems that they find oppressive or overly formal and bureaucratic and which render them powerless. For many, the result is avoidance of such systems or situations and a deep distrust and wariness of those who represent positions of authority.

Staff at Safespace responded to these individuals' barriers to learning by:

- **Providing a learning environment that was different to previous models of power and authority that the young people had experienced.** Brightly coloured areas which publicly displayed people's work and using first names were strategies employed by teachers at Safespace to signal this different approach. All levels of staff, including the Connexions advisor, worked hard to ensure that the young people felt listened to and that their opinions were valued.
- **Being 'firm but fair'.** Workers at Safespace understood the experiences of violence and bullying in the lives of the young people they worked with. As a result they operated a framework that was 'firm but fair', recognising that anything else would lead to further disengagement.

This approach was not always found to be easy to implement. Sometimes, for example, what an individual wanted or needed was in direct conflict with the smooth running and values of the centre. However, understanding these issues makes it possible for a provider to be flexible and responsive to the needs of the learner. This is demonstrated, for example, by Sophie's teachers, who supported her wider learning interests in poetry and expressive writing.

Example of Guideline 3: Take account of people's feelings of social exclusion

Although people sometimes feel 'different' and outside of things, it is possible to have aspirations and a strong sense of the future as well, shown in Steve's life.

Library photo, posed by models ©Serghei Starus/Shutterstock

Steve was in his early 30s when we met him. He said that he hated his 'authoritarian' school as it felt clinical and abrupt. His dyslexia was not diagnosed and he went through what he found to be a harsh system with no support. His aggressive response to people laughing when he tried to read aloud got him into trouble and he started skipping school regularly from the age of 13. Steve felt that many people like him who got into trouble had experienced authoritarian schools and teachers – he felt that was a significant factor in this behaviour.

By 20 years old he dabbled in drugs and became addicted to hard drugs. He started stealing to feed his habit and was sent to prison for theft. On release he stole again to buy drugs and was sentenced to a further five years. He managed to make a fresh start by moving to London when his girlfriend had a baby, but moved back to the North West when his mother became ill. Upon return, he became involved in drugs again, resulting in the baby being taken into care by social services. Eventually Steve and his girlfriend got married, had another baby and stopped using drugs. He became involved in a local group to support people on drugs.

Although his writing skills were poor as a consequence of his dyslexia, he did not want to engage with the discrete literacy provision offered at Pandion Hall. He did not see it as important, and did not want to repeat the negative learning experiences of his childhood. He enjoyed the structured day programme as he was able to learn whilst doing activities: he found what he was learning interesting and useful to his life. Steve also found the support and safety of the programme important to his ability to participate, as he was not likely to bump into old acquaintances from his drug-using days.

Steve's everyday literacy and numeracy practices

Steve used literacy in his everyday life for travelling on public transport, for keeping in contact with family and friends and for knowing what was going on in his community. He struggled with official texts due to his dyslexia, but was able take family decisions and use his skills to build a new and more stable family unit.

Steve used his literacy to manage his continued success in coming off drugs. He also used numeracy to manage his money.

People's feelings are central to their experiences, past, present and planned. A sense of future was important to nearly everyone that we spoke to. People told of things that they hoped to achieve: a good job, somewhere decent to live, good health and a settled home life. Many of these aspirations indicated that people wanted to have more control over their environment and circumstances, in contrast to unpredictable events in their own and their family's lives. Sometimes people had a clear sense of the path that led to this future, such as getting qualifications, 'drying out', leaving a violent relationship or finding employment. For example, Sophie wanted to take GCSE and A Level exams to enable her to follow her career path in veterinary nursing. Others had a less clearly developed path, and spoke just of 'moving forward'.

Whilst there was a connection with learning as a route to achieving future goals, it was less often directly linked to gaining qualifications. This could be an indication of a lack of confidence about managing a course through to achieving a qualification. Steve's life story shows how moving towards a future takes many paths and some detours. Sometimes it moves straight ahead and then, as life circumstances intervene, it changes direction, appearing at times to go backwards. Over time, however, it is clear that he worked towards setting and achieving his own goals and eventually was successful. The time taken for him to achieve this was longer than usual for a typical adult LLN course. This is an important feature of learning in community settings – that it takes longer and requires flexibility and resourcefulness.

Implications for teaching and learning

Steve's priority was 'a clean, healthy life' and with that foundation he felt he could achieve other things that were important to him. His engagement with learning was tied to the ability to work towards his own and his family's future. Whilst Steve's idea of the future might have changed as a result of events and circumstances, such as being in prison, having a baby and his mother's illness, he was nevertheless holding on to the sense that at some point it would be possible to construct something positive. This was a powerful motivator for him and recognised by those who taught him.

The following points may help socially excluded people to achieve future goals:

- **When lives are in transition, learning can offer a bridge to a more stable future.** Many of those who attended Pandion Hall and Safespace were in a process of transition. They were moving from and between different circumstances – sometimes feeling in control and sometimes not. Where LLN learning was seen as having purpose and relevance to achieving a desired future, people engaged and persisted with it. Caroline, as we saw, wanted to work in an office. Taking literacy or numeracy courses would enable her to achieve a concrete aim: in spite of ongoing difficulties, she persisted. Sophie was also motivated to improve her literacy and numeracy skills as she needed these to be able to study up to A Levels – her passport to entering her desired career. She maintained a desire and commitment to study once her circumstances allowed. She saw herself as an interrupted learner rather than as a failed one. Steve's sense of the future was expressed in more general terms. For him it was 'being healthy' and not drug-dependent. He, too, moved forward: he started working as a community research assistant at a local university, taking steps towards planning and achieving a concrete and immediate future.

- **Provide a supportive, non-judgemental learning environment where privacy is maintained.** People described their reluctance to tell those in formal education classes what they were dealing with or to explain absences. Caroline, above, explained that she kept her drinking hidden at college and did not explain why she did not attend classes regularly.

Similarly, women we spoke to from the domestic violence support group kept their experiences hidden as they did not want to be labelled or judged by this aspect of their lives. This was compounded by the frequent disruption of having to move, to attend court, or by regular social workers or other officials' visits. Where people were managing hidden and, they felt, 'spoiled' identities, it created intense anxiety in formal provision. This often resulted in complete withdrawal. It was neither the course content nor the ability to study, but the difficultly of fitting in with the regular attendance patterns and implicit assumptions with which they struggled.

People often described themselves as not being part of 'normal' life, of being different and an outsider. One of the most significant benefits at Pandion Hall for Caroline and others was not needing to explain themselves. As everyone was there for similar reasons, less had to be hidden or publicly managed. A sense of belonging and acceptance, based on being different to others with more regular lives, was important for the young people at Safespace. For the women at Emerge, who had often been isolated, finding out that they were not the only ones living with violence was hugely significant. Those who were attending college valued the recognition and support they received from the domestic violence support group, which enabled them to continue, whatever the difficulties.

■ **Being different need not always be negative.** People spoke of what they gained by seeing life differently and engaging positively with different life experiences. For Caroline, being 'normal' meant being part of what she stereotyped as 'golf playing, holding dinner parties, happy families'. Members of the tenants' association expressed great pride and satisfaction in being independent and able to 'do things for themselves'. This was in contrast to the slower and impenetrable bureaucracies that they frequently dealt with, which they felt were inefficient and did not take account of their needs. Belonging to a voluntary organisation, run independently for the benefit of their community and clients, offered them a source of pride and continuing motivation. They felt they were able to contribute something uniquely different which had a positive impact on their estate.

Example of Guideline 4: Recognise and acknowledge people's existing skills and competencies

Although people may struggle at some point in their life to succeed in learning, for a variety of reasons, they may have had previous successful learning experiences. Teresa shows how some people may have a long learning career with many ups and downs.

Library photo, posed by models
©iofoto/Shutterstock

Teresa had a difficult family upbringing. She described herself as the 'black sheep' of the family, not doing well at school and 'sleeping around' at an early age. She was regularly bullied and beaten up as a child, living in a close-knit community, but one in which both children and adults used violence. She had a serious relationship between the ages of 15 and 21 which was violent. Although at the time she did not find it frightening, it resulted in her becoming homeless. Despite earlier school failure and living in a difficult relationship Teresa went back to college and achieved an O Level in English and did a First Diploma in Business Studies. She had to leave the course after the break-up of her relationship as she was homeless with a child to support.

She was offered office work but was unable to keep office hours because of childcare problems. She lacked support at home and she worked in several chip shops. A new partner also became violent and the effect of this, another child and the lack of support to study resulted in her giving up the new college course in electronics that she had started. Having left college, she became involved in drugs, ending up homeless because of lack of money and rent arrears.

Teresa left this relationship and went to live with her mother. This provided her with somewhere to live as well as help with the children, and enabled Teresa to work in a care home and become financially independent. The arrangement was stressful as Teresa felt that her son suffered from ADS (Attention Deficit Syndrome) and her mother was unable to care for him properly. She also feared that he was becoming violent like his father. Emerge supported her application for a house of her own and provided emotional support for her difficulties with her children. Teresa ended up leaving work as she did not have sufficiently reliable childcare for a job that required shifts and anti-social hours. She was learning to use the computer that Emerge had provided whilst she was off work. Through using the computer, she was learning new skills and at the same time helping Emerge with their administration.

Teresa's everyday literacy and numeracy practices

Teresa had used literacy to set up and run several homes after being made homeless. She read and searched the web for information about her son's ADH condition so that she could support him and discuss this with his school. She used literacy in her voluntary work for Chrysalis and added to her IT skills by working in their office and borrowing a computer to practise at home. Teresa was also keen to support her son's literacy and IT learning so that he would have more chances than she has had.

Teresa used numeracy skills to manage several periods of debt arising from her drug dependency. She managed her finances and negotiated with the benefits office and the bank.

Despite unpredictable and difficult circumstances and events, the people we spoke to continued to learn throughout their lives. There were many instances of new skills being added to existing ones, learned from a friend or in a non-educational setting such as a pub. People routinely used their skills and knowledge to deal with the benefit system, negotiate the legal or care systems or to manage their health. Although many would be categorised as non-learners or 'hard to reach' learners, this 'label' often only reflected one point or episode in their lives and related only to formal learning.

Many people practised and enjoyed writing, including poetry or rap, doing crosswords or keeping a diary. Others enjoyed reading: about music, hobbies or sport. They clearly were learning, and using a variety of languages, literacies and numeracies in their everyday lives. Recognising the meaning and value of informal learning inside formal learning environments enables learners to build on what they already know, positioning them as people who can and do already learn. Although dealing with many difficulties, Teresa carried on learning.

Implications for teaching and learning

Teresa's story demonstrates the complexity in adults' lives and how circumstances and events interact with each other. It also shows how positive change and steps to take control of one's life can sometimes go backwards. Nonetheless, by **creating opportunities for people to use and develop their existing skills,** the following providers helped people to get back and remain on track.

The practice at Emerge and The Big Issue is to talk to people about their existing skills and competencies as well as their 'pressing needs'. Through finding out what Teresa could already do, Emerge was able to provide a computer for her to practise on at home, providing the opportunity for her to gain confidence and brush up her skills. As she was not able to attend a college course, the supported, self-directed learning they offered made learning possible. As her confidence improved, workers at Emerge asked her to undertake routine administrative tasks, enabling her to feel valued by the centre and learn more skills. Teresa spoke about attending the local drop-in centre to build on her new experience in an IT and spelling class. She said it was important to be recognised for what she could do rather than concentrating on the difficult aspects of her life, and this was something that the support workers and teachers were able to do.

At The Big Issue, several of the people attending IT and numeracy classes had existing qualifications, some up to degree level. The teachers established what existing skills people had, including different types of writing and the ability to use the computer for information-gathering and leisure. These skills and knowledge were used to develop new skills which people wanted to learn. For some, the aim was to develop self-expression and to be able to communicate effectively socially with others. For others, learning included activities such as music and arts where people already had skills, knowledge and interests to build on. Music technology was used at The Big Issue and Pandion Hall whilst free writing was used at Safespace and Emerge. Art was used, in some form, by each organisation.

3 Supporting adult literacy, numeracy and ESOL teaching in community settings

This section describes how the insights from the research can be translated into practice. Possibilities and challenges are explored, taking account of the complexity and tensions involved. Some issues relate to local factors and particular contexts. Others respond to national circumstances, such as ensuring sustainability in learning within the funding available.

Possibilities and challenges

Some learners do want to access mainstream provision and to participate in formal learning; however, they need confidence and support to attend. For example, Emerge actively helped women to attend a local college, and Pandion Hall helped Caroline. For others, attending college was a step too far. They did not yet see the relevance in their lives of learning subjects called language, literacy or numeracy, or life was too turbulent to attend classes on a regular basis.

Learning in organisations such as Pandion Hall, Safespace and The Big Issue was successful when it fitted, or was embedded within, the organisation's existing flexible and creative ways of working. People attending classes there did not have to pretend they were 'normal': it was already established that they were dealing with difficult factors. Both tutors and other professionals were aware of their current circumstances and often, too, the histories people brought to learning. People did not have to develop new relationships involving issues of power and trust with those providing the learning opportunities, as these were part and parcel of the process of negotiating participation. Absences, whether for recuperation, attending court or resulting from being made homeless, did not have to be explained or accounted for.

Learning that was embedded within the organisation's systems for support and core areas of service delivery worked well, even when courses or activities were delivered by tutors from a college. The content, delivery and time frames for learning activity were adapted to fit the core support services being provided. In addition, people felt safe within these environments. Their emotional experiences and reactions were accepted as part of their identity and behaviour. It was accepted that learning sometimes had to be suspended, if someone was too

Discussing matters informally
Library photo, posed by models ©*www.JohnBirdsall.co.uk*

preoccupied with immediate concerns and just needed a cup of tea and a chat.
When people were too distressed or preoccupied, they were not going to learn.
Where external tutors delivered courses without responding similarly to these
factors, they were less successful. They were successful where they were able to
adapt to the host organisation's environment, fitting in with its ethos, and
respecting that the place of learning in people's lives might not be as a first or
even second priority.

Successful tutors offered learners a bridge to cross over what was felt to be a
big divide, enabling them to progress to more formal provision in college.

Dipping in and out

Many learners in our research sites 'dipped in and out 'of learning; they attended
for a while, left before completing courses and then returned to learning. The
young people at the homeless shelter often attended for a short while but then
stopped coming as their circumstances changed. Whilst this might be recorded
on a college register as a 'drop out', many of the young people felt that even
attending for a short while counted as a success. This was similar for women at
the domestic violence support group and for homeless adults at The Big Issue –
they knew that it was circumstances that constrained their attendance, rather
than their commitment. Many like Sophie described it as interrupted learning
rather than dropping out or failing.

Different perceptions and practices about patterns of attendance are significant. It is critical to understand why some people find accessing learning more difficult than others – they are working on a different time scale. Rather than being 'hard to reach', it is set time scales and timetables set that are out of their reach, making regular attendance, and therefore success, difficult to achieve.

The 'right time'

Making learning opportunities available at the 'right time' in an individual's life was recognised by many in our study as important in gaining people's interest. The 'right time'...

- emerges from a combination of life experiences, including current circumstances and events, individual goals and the support available to sustain participation
- can be triggered when learning opportunities are identified which can be used as a bridge between a person's immediate priorities and their longer-term goals.

For example, Sophie's life was shaped by the immediate need for safe housing and structure in her life, which had made attending formal learning impossible to sustain. Although learning was part of her longer-term goals, it was not the right time to start. Safespace worked flexibly with Sophie's rapidly changing circumstances, providing support and informal learning activities that proved more successful at that moment. They recognised that circumstances, more than ability or motivation, would influence the 'right time' for Sophie to participate in formal learning.

For others like Steve and Caroline, the 'right time' to learn was when drug and alcohol dependency became controlled. In Steve's case, the right time depended on being 'clean and healthy'. For Caroline, it was a matter of managing to have enough confidence to attend college without needing to drink to deal with the anxiety.

The 'right time' is not the end point in a linear process of managing difficult circumstances. Teresa's life shows that the 'right time' to learn can become the 'wrong time', as events change priorities and the ability to participate. Learning was successful when teachers were able to offer it at the 'right time' for the individual.

Linking the curriculum with learners' lives

It is important to understand which existing skills and competencies can be linked to the curriculum and which cannot. Whilst people are often comfortable and confident with informal learning, it can be useful to show learners how some of these skills are also valued within formal qualification structures. Experienced teachers described using the curriculum in a multifaceted and multimodal way. They may use visual, sound, text or speech media to support speaking and listening. One example given was the benefit of a life history approach with a 60-plus age group and with gypsy and traveller groups, where oral traditions are valued and practised in everyday life within communities. Other examples include linking the adult curriculum with what children are learning at school, particularly in Year 7, where both parents and children learned about Shakespeare. For the parents, this was linked to speaking and listening in the adult curriculum where such learning could be accredited.

In some circumstances, group work was used as an effective catalyst for learning. It provided models and positive examples of people 'having a go and achieving' something for themselves. Teachers reported instances of where this generated healthy rivalry. However, other teachers felt that group work could be a source of friction and even confrontation where local disputes came into the classroom. Creating and maintaining a safe environment was essential and many organisations' rules for groups included bans on alcohol and drugs and taking time out to deal with anger. It was important to maintain these rules within learning environments and teachers emphasised the need to learn people management skills in initial training and continuing development. Those teachers who came from a community development or regeneration background felt that their training and experiences prepared them for teaching in community environments. They felt this was lacking in adult LLN teacher training and CPD. Other teachers without this background said they learned 'on the job'. This was often felt to be unsatisfactory for the complex issues they were dealing with and the equally complex responses they needed to make.

Some teachers felt that although it was possible to use the core curriculum creatively, particularly by using speaking and listening, there was still a challenge to make sure teaching and learning to the curriculum offered meaning and relevance to people's lives. This challenge is part of a continuing debate about how LLN skills are understood and taught, and the purposes and meanings they have in people's lives (Green and Howard 2007): how to value recognition of achievement, skills and gaining qualifications, and also value developing the social practices and social confidence associated with using literacy and numeracy as part of life.

Teaching and learning: using social practice pedagogy

In the past, teacher training and professional development have varied in the extent of their focus on community settings. However, from September 2007 it will be expected that all new teachers gain experience in more than one context and teacher-trainers should be urged to include community learning in their initial and CPD programmes. It is essential to consider the diversity and wide range of learners' needs and purposes (Appleby, 2007). We need to continually ask: what makes teaching in the community different and how can we best respond to the people who come to this type of provision?

Funders, teachers and providers need to be clear about what can realistically be achieved within a standard 30-hour or other defined course parameters in organisations and in areas where social and health problems proliferate. One teacher commented of her environment: 'nobody is well, everyone is ill'. Health is often a major factor for those living in poverty, with bad housing, physical or mental illness or disabilities, and few material resources. It is difficult to attend regularly whilst managing chronic ill-health alongside other problems. Research shows that people studying below Entry 2 are more affected by health factors than those in the general population (Bynner and Parsons, 2006, 2007). Teachers working in community settings felt that to achieve qualifications, including those within the national targets, inside the time constraints of many courses was 'asking for a miracle'. It was also observed that, in these settings particularly, self-confidence takes many more than 30 hours to improve after what has sometimes been a lifetime of feeling defeated. The shift required in moving from what was described as an overwhelming 'everybody is crap' attitude, towards identifying oneself as a learner with potential to grow, needs both time and support. Progress in learning (measured by a rise in the level attainment) may take years rather than months, and recognising small steps in attainment is critical.

Teachers can celebrate diversity, avoiding stereotypes or potentially patronising language, for example, about 'non-traditional' or 'hard to reach' groups. It is important to explore diversity and difference even when learners and potential learners may feel themselves to be outsiders or socially excluded. Teachers in our study aimed to create safe spaces where everyone was listened to, accepted and valued. This was often challenging. It included dealing with ongoing conflict between people who attended class, tackling racist or homophobic comments and developing group rules that were respected and adhered to.

Getting the right balance in classroom management required a mixture of authority and care to establish a safe, constructive environment. Activities ranged from discussing anger management to bringing a chocolate cake to class every week. The 'chocolate cake approach' was recognised as a serious aspect of good practice, particularly when working with people with few personal resources or luxury in their lives.

Flexible provision: what counts as learning

Some teachers found that what they were able to offer was too limited to be relevant to the needs of learners. Those who had a community regeneration background and who had then trained as literacy and ESOL teachers felt that they were working with a 'one size fits all' model of learning that did not easily fit a community wide-brief.

However, teachers described various ways of 'hooking' learners, either initially or to help sustain attendance. Two examples of this are:

- Finding ways of including as learning the time that refugee and asylum-seekers spent outside the classroom.
- Seeking funding through local partnerships with primary health care trusts and other development agencies. The challenge is to maintain continuity. Refugee and asylum-seekers' additional language and literacy needs in dealing with complex legal and health care systems fell between several areas of funding and legal responsibilities – e.g. education, housing, health and the Home Office. With leadership, management and vision, it is possible to join up services across these areas, to include and benefit many people deemed to be 'at risk' or 'vulnerable'.

Teachers who worked in support agencies recognised that people at risk and living with formidable problems have 'normal' aspirations. While prioritising support for coping and managing strategies, they looked at what LLN meant in the classroom and in people's lives, registering skills people already possessed and practised and building on them. They broke tasks down into small achievable steps so that learners could see progress.

Responsive teaching and ethical issues

Finding out about the lives of the learners was a key to building on successful managing strategies or helping to developing new ones. This required listening carefully to where each person felt they were 'coming from' and where they 'wanted to go'. Some teachers used tools such as Individual Learning Plans (ILPs) to discuss and record progress related to the curriculum. For others, this did not sufficiently capture on its own the informal learning in which people were engaged. They therefore used a variety of ways of working with individuals to show increases, or decreases, in confidence, social participation, persisting with attendance or reflecting on learning and barriers thereto. These included written records, notebooks, discussion, free writing, poetry or photography.

Not all attendance in learning is voluntary or free-standing. For example, going to a Family Learning course could be part of a formal care plan. Where several agencies and services are involved in provision (e.g. Children Services or the Home Office), there are issues to be aware of in keeping records, or disclosure. There is the need to carefully negotiate what can be kept confidential and what cannot. For example, there is the possibility that learning material could be used as 'evidence' in child abuse or asylum cases. Most service providers have a duty under the Children Act (1989) and, more recently, Every Child Matters, to report concerns of child safety.

The following issues emerged as important practice for teachers working with priority groups:

- not to promise confidentiality when this cannot be achieved.
- to develop active networks of professionals in other fields so learners can be referred to those with appropriate expertise, as necessary.
- to maintain professional boundaries to prevent burn out and overload, as well as to ensure advice and support are offered within the teacher's role and the limits of his/her professional expertise.
- to create networks of other teachers in other contexts for information sharing and support to lessen isolation.

Supporting learners as people

The roles and responsibilities of people who come to learn need to be taken into account. They may be parents, carers, interpreters, volunteers, workers, church members, community elders, mentors and advice workers. Sometimes these roles make attendance in the familiarity of their own local environment or community the most meaningful and attractive setting. For community regeneration projects, learning can be embedded within wider activities connected to a local community. Community-based environments can offer support and a sense of safety to particular groups, including women, minority ethnic communities, or faith groups.

Where provision in the community is organised by support agencies, such as Pandion Hall and Safespace, mechanisms are often in place to discover and support individuals' particular roles and responsibilities – for example, Caroline's responsibilities as a mother and Sophie's as an expectant mother. This is also the case in residential provision: an example was given of a residential college for adult with disabilities.

A successful approach to learning in organisations where the core purpose is, for example, drug dependency or homelessness, is to establish networks and groups. Where provision is embedded within community projects, this often means building a new group from scratch. As Veronica McGivney (2000) has shown, outreach work is a vital part of this process, and requires funding support. Teachers and regeneration workers gave examples of developing activities such as cooking or dancing which enabled people to get to know others and to form a group who wanted to learn together. From this, the place, time and frequency of a programme could be negotiated to fit in with life patterns, purposes, interests and commitments. An established group of Asian women learners already knew exactly what they wanted, when and where. They asked for an ESOL class in the early afternoon, so as not to clash with picking up children and cooking the family meal, to take place in a group member's house. They simply requested a suitable tutor.

Reducing barriers to learning

Provision within the community offers a positive option for some people who cannot manage other types of provision. For access to main-site college provision, learners need money for bus fares, additional time, and sometimes a crèche. For part-time employed staff to access workplace learning, it has to be available to them at times that fit with their working hours.

However, the fact that a learning programme is located in the community does not guarantee that it will be flexible or in itself meet people's needs. There may be specific or local barriers to participation, such as:

- real, physical barriers, e.g. a busy dual carriageway without a safe crossing
- mixed-gendered environments or programmes that ignore important religious events.

Teachers also need to ensure that:

- learners can contribute their own experiences
- learners are treated with respect
- learning programmes, where based on national curricula, are adapted to be as relevant and useful to their particular learners as possible.

A successful approach also includes a strong commitment to democratic learning, social inclusion and citizenship (Coare and Johnston, 2003; Stuart and Thomson, 2002). These principles are often explicit in community organisations which support LLN learning.

Many community educators, and those involved in community regeneration, may already be sensitive to the structural nature of educational and social inequality, have a critical understanding of how different literacies and numeracies are developed and defined by more, or less, powerful social groups; and understand how they are used, and for what purposes. This understanding needs to be developed in teacher education and CPD for all those working in LLN community settings (Crowther, Tett and Hamilton, 2001), and the many new teachers and organisations engaged in LLN.

Why people attend

Some people want to learn specific skills such as spelling or fractions because they had not acquired them when young and wanted to feel good learning them as an adult. For others, there are particular skills they need in order to progress onto college or into employment. Often people come with a general aim to 'do computers' and develop new skills, e.g. in graphics or designing sound systems. For some people, to learn about learning itself and how to become an independent learner is a key starting point.

The ALL research showed that it was important that those people who already knew what they wanted were given the opportunity to achieve this, as well as to extend their skills and knowledge. Learners who were less clear about the relevance of what they wanted to learn for their future needed encouragement and careful advice to explore this, whilst achieving short-term aims. Several teachers described the many small steps that adults need to take at the beginning of a new learning journey (Ward and Edwards, 2002).

For some people, learning is at first primarily about having a safe environment, which helps them hold their lives together. Such an environment offers:

- a structure and focus to the day
- new networks of support which extend into other areas of life
- safety from bullying and verbal and physical harassment
- someone to listen to fears and anxieties
- help with practical difficulties
- food or shelter from bad weather.

Conclusion

This guide has offered research findings, principles and guidance on teaching and learning adult LLN in community settings. It has looked at how this type of provision can differ from that in the college sector or workplace. We have used a social practice approach, which connects people's lives with their learning. This allows teachers to build on some of the factors that shape people's lives – their life histories, current circumstances and futures. This perspective sheds light on how formal learning may often be out of the reach of some people: it is not the potential learners who are 'hard to reach' (Howard, 2001). Classroom-based learning is often outside the grasp of those with the least material or social resources in society. Community organisations can offer access to many otherwise excluded groups.

People come to learn for many reasons and learn in diverse ways, through a range of community-based organisations focusing on groups with particular needs and problems. Most adult LLN is offered in the FE sector, often in colleges or workplace learning; but people identified in the Skills for Life strategy as priority groups may be those least likely to engage with their provision. Many experience social exclusion and attend adult LLN in community settings as the first step towards inclusion.

Adult community learning organisations have recognised and responded to the adults and young people who learn in these settings. Their teaching strategies are distinct and varied, and need to learn continuously how best to provide flexible, relevant and adequately supported learning in a demanding environment. Teacher education and CPD providers need to develop the skills, capabilities and qualities of teachers and other professionals in this sector.

The case studies of the four learners in this guide show how people do engage and persist in learning in spite of unusually difficult circumstances and events in their lives. They learn and make progress. For some, it may take significant periods of time, often interrupted. Learning happens when the person feels he or she is at the 'right time' to learn. Flexible methods used to teach useful skills whilst providing structure are essential to support motivation, success and a better future.

References

Appleby, Y. (2007) 'Who are the learners?' In N. Hughes and I.Schwab (eds), *Skills for Life: Teaching Adult Literacy*. Milton Keynes: Open University Press. This chapter discusses how people become categorised as learners, even when they might not describe themselves in this way.

Appleby, Y. and Barton, D. (2008 forthcoming) *Responding to people's lives*, Leicester: NIACE/NRDC. This short guide draws upon recent research that looked at literacy, language and numeracy teaching in college settings. It provides examples from the classroom and in collaboration with practitioners and suggests ways of applying these to practice, discussing the accompanying challenges.

Barton, D., Appleby, Y., Hodge, R., Tusting, K. and Ivanič, R (2006) *Relating adults' lives and learning: participation and engagement in different settings*, London: NRDC. This is a report from the Adult Learners' Lives (ALL) research project which looked at adults' lives and LLN learning in different community settings.

Barton, D. and Hamilton, M. (2000) *Local Literacies: Reading and Writing in One Community*, London: Routledge. Local Literacies provides detail of how people use LLN in their everyday lives, developed into a social practice approach. It uses cases studies to illustrate how people's passions, uses and meanings are located in their everyday practices.

Bynner, J. and Parsons, S. (2006) *New Light on Literacy and Numeracy* London: NRDC. This report draws upon data from the British cohort studies, which chart the lives of a sample of people born in certain years. This report shows the strong links between low levels of literacy and numeracy and aspects of social deprivation and social exclusion.

Coare, P. and Johnston, R. (eds) (2003) *Adult learning, citizenship and community voices: Exploring community based practice*. Leicester: NIACE. This collection explores ways of achieving adult education that has a baseline of social justice, economic equality and critical democracy. Contributions explore practice as well as policy issues from the perspective of working in the community.

Crowther, J., Hamilton, M., Tett, L. (eds) (2001) *Powerful Literacies*. Leicester: NIACE. This collection makes visible the often hidden aspects of power in literacy. It challenges the orthodoxy of seeing literacy as skills for economic growth by highlighting inequalities and that way that literacy can be used to disempower people.

Deer Richardson, L. and Wolfe, M. (eds) (2004) *Principles and Practice of Informal Education: Learning through life*. London: Routledge. This collection arises from the authors work with the YMCA George Williams College's distance learning BA. It explores the principles and practice of informal education in areas including youth work and community and adult education.

DfEE (2001) *Skills for Life: The national strategy for improving adult literacy and numeracy skills*. London: Department for Education and Employment. This document lays out the *Skills for Life* strategy.

Green, A. and Howard, U. (2007) *Skills and social practices: making common cause*. London: NRDC. Drawing on research evidence from NRDC and other sources, this paper identifies how social practices and skills-based approaches can be mutually supportive, coming together in teaching strategies, assessment and classroom relationships to help learners develop in many different aspects of their lives.

Hamilton, M. and Hillier, Y. (2006) *A history of adult literacy, numeracy and ESOL 1970 –2000*. Stoke-on-Trent: Trentham Books. The authors provide a recent history (preceding the *Skills for Life* strategy) showing the changes to the field of adult basic education and adult literacy. It shows how definitions, target population and initiatives changed in this thirty-year period when 'illiteracy' became defined as a national problem.

Horsman, J. (2000) *Too Scared to Learn: Women, Violence and Education*. New Jersey: Lawrence Erlbaum. Jenny Horsman's work, carried out with practitioners in Canada, shows the impact of violence on the lives of learners. She found that people were unable to concentrate, were fearful for their safety and were unconfident in most aspects of their lives. Many practitioners reported that they were unaware of this in the lives of their learners, and several acknowledged it was an issue for them.

Howard, U. (2001) 'Stimulating Demand for Learning: An ideas paper on attracting new learners'. London: LSDA. This paper explores concepts of 'hard to reach' learners and ways of looking at the learning infrastructure from learners' perspectives.

Ivanič, R., Appleby, Y., Hodge, R., Tusting, K. and Barton, D. (2006) *Linking Learning and Everyday Life: A social perspective on Adult Language, Literacy and Numeracy classes.* London: NRDC. This is the second report from the Adult Learners' Lives (ALL) research project. It described research carried out in adult LLN classes and the relationship of this learning to what people did in their everyday lives.

McGivney, V. (2000) *Discovering Outreach: Concepts, issues and practices,* Leicester: NIACE. This work draws upon a wide range of sources describing the meaning and significance of outreach work, particularly working to provide community-based learning opportunities and collaborating with other services and agencies. The study concludes that, although effective in widening participation, it requires a substantial investment which is not always available.

McNeil, B. and Dixon, L. (2005) *Success factors in informal learning: young adults' experiences of literacy, language and numeracy.* London: NRDC. This work reports findings from a project, jointly carried out by NRDC and the Young Adults Learning Partnership (YALP), on the contribution of informal education to the development of socially-excluded young adults' LLN skills.

Papen, U. (2005) *Adult Literacy as Social Practice: More than skills.* London: Routledge. This book, designed to support an adult LLN distance-learning course at Lancaster University, provides a clear description of a social practice approach. It has guided readings from a range of authors – from describing work on the streets of South Africa to discussing how to conduct literacy as social practice research.

Reder, S. (2004) Keynote address, NRDC International Conference, Nottingham. Steve Reder used the term 'turbulence' to describe the difficulties and irregularities some people experience in their lives. That is based upon research in America carried out by National Center for the Study of Adult Learning and Literacy (NCSALL).

Stuart, M. and Thomson, A. (eds) (2002) *Engaging with difference: The 'other' in Adult Education.* Leicester: NIACE. This collection focuses on attempts in adult education to engage with the learning needs of individuals and groups who are marginalised and have been excluded by the education system. They use the concept of 'other' to describe ways in which people and communities make sense of being different and discuss the complexities for educators engaging with 'difference'.

Tett, L. (2006) *Community Education, Lifelong Learning and Social Inclusion (second edition)*, Edinburgh: Dunedin Academic Press. This book describes definitions and bodies of knowledge associated with community education. The examples are drawn from Scotland but the tensions discussed between education in the community and community development are more widely applicable.

Ward, J. and Edwards, J. (2002) *Learning Journeys: Learners' Voices*. London: LSDA. This accessible book describes a practitioner research project that supported tutors to understand both barriers and progress in student learning by using the metaphor of a journey. This method enabled students to use familiar everyday language to express the feelings about learning or their lack of progress.

Further reading

Auerbach, E. with Barahona, B., Midy, J., Vaqueroano, F., Zambrano, A. and Arnaud, J. (1996) *From The Community to the Community: A Guidebook for Participatory Literacy Training.* New Jersey: Lawrence Erlbaum. This source book draws upon the recognition that communities themselves are sources, and can be producers, of knowledge. It uses a participatory model of working with participants to develop resources for teaching English as a second language, rooted in local communities.

Colley, H., Hodkinson, P. and Malcolm, J. (2003) *Informality and formality in learning: a report for the Learning and Skills Research Centre.* London: Learning and Skills Research Centre. This report provides a rich source of information, examples and discussion around models of formal, non-formal and informal learning.

Grief, S., Murphy, H., Nijjar, B. and Taylor, C. (2002) *Opening up a new world: A good practice guide for delivering basic skills and ESOL in the local community.* This short booklet provides insights for practice from a FEFC initiative, carried out by NIACE and the LSDA, to support community ESOL learning. It explores issues such as engaging new learners, partnership work, staff development, recording outcomes and using IT.

Hillage, J., Uden, T., Aldridge, F. and Eccles, J. (2000) *Adult Learning in England.* Leicester: NIACE. This book provides a useful review of adult learning in England. It covers areas such as participation, motivation, needs and provision, widening participation and returns from learning.

Howard, U. (2007) 'Sides to middle – adult learning is for everyone' in A. Tuckett (ed.), *Participation and the pursuit of equality: Essays in adult learning, widening participation and achievement.* Leicester: NIACE. This chapter contributed to the current debates about the scale and scope of the *Skills for Life* strategy. It suggests that paradoxically those who are defined by the strategy as in most need find it most difficult to access provision, especially learners at or below Entry 2.

Jude, C. (2003) *Consulting Adults.* Leicester: NIACE. This short booklet tackles the issues of how to involve adults as equal partners in adult learning provision. It covers working in partnership, researching and consulting as well as building sustainability within programmes.

Lambe, T., Mark, R., Murphy, P., Soroke, B. (2006) *Literacy, Equality and Creativity: Resources Guide for Adult Learners*, Belfast: School of Education, Queen's University, Belfast. This book from The Literacy and Equality in Irish Society (LEIS) provides ideas and resources for creative work with adults aimed at working towards social inclusion.

McGivney, V. (2006) *Adult Learning at a Glance*, Leicester: NIACE. This is a valuable source book that provides a digest of facts and figures for people working in adult learning. It focuses on three main areas: the UK population, the labour market and education and training, showing changes and trends.

Taylor, D. (1996) *Toxic Literacies: Exposing the Injustice of Bureaucratic Texts.* Portsmouth NH: Heinemann. This book shows the impact of bureaucratic texts in the lives of four people who live on the margins of American society. It shows the barriers that people face in learning, such as drug addiction and alcohol dependency, whilst telling their stories in a powerful and accessible way.

Wilson, A., Robertshaw, L. (2006) *Epic: Engaging People in Change*, Doncaster: DARTS. This short and engaging booklet describes the EPIC project in Doncaster which worked with a number of local community groups funded through a Neighbourhood Renewal Fund grant. It provides examples of creative work and outlines helpful points that support the work for others to follow.

Resources and websites

Australian Council for Adult Literacy	http://www.acal.edu.au
Communities Scotland	http://www.lc.communitiesscotland.gov.uk
Lancaster Literacy Research Centre (LLRC)	http://www.literacy.lancaster.ac.uk
Lifelong Learning UK (LLUK), for the 2007+ professional standards for teachers and requirements for a range of teaching practice experience	http://www.lluk.org
National Adult Literacy Agency (NALA) in Ireland	http://www.nala.ie
National Basic Skills Strategy for Wales	http://www.basic-skills-observatory-wales.org
National Center for the Study of Adult Learning and Literacy (NCSALL) in the US Strategy	http://www.ncsall.net
National Institute of Adult Continuing Education (NIACE)	http://www.niace.org.uk
National Literacy Trust	http://www.literacytrust.org.uk
National Research and Development Centre for Adult Literacy, Numeracy and ESOL (NRDC)	http://www.nrdc.org.uk
Research and Practice in Adult Literacy (RaPAL)	http://www.rapal.org.uk
Read, Write Plus (DCSF)	http://www.dfes.gov.uk
Research in Practice in Adult Literacy (RiPAL) in Canada	http://www.nald.ca
Talent	http://www.talent.ac.uk
The Basic Skills Agency (BSA)	http://www.basic-skills.co.uk
The Network for Workplace Language, Literacy and Numeracy	http://www.thenetwork.co.uk